Coffee and Coffeehouses

A Local and International History

Chatgris Press
P.O. Box 15092
New Orleans, LA 70175-5092

© Copyright 1999 by Gary Michael Smith. All rights reserved.

No part of this work may be reproduced in any form or transmitted by any means—performance, graphic, electronic, or mechanical, including photocopying, recording, taping, filming, information storage and retrieval systems, or posting on Internet websites—without written permission from the author.

ISBN 0-9658380-2-1

Printed in the United States of America

This book was developed using Corel Corporation WordPerfect 7.0 for Windows 95. The cover art is Corel Clipart. The text and cover production work was provided by TLC, Inc. in Metairie, LA. The fonts used are Times New Roman, Arial, Arial Narrow, Script MT Bold, and Lucida Calligraphy.

Contents

Contents   iii
Tables   iv
Dedication   v
Acknowledgments   vi
From the Author   vii

Part 1 - A History Lesson

The History of Coffee   3
The History of Coffeehouses   7
Early Coffee-Making   10
Early Coffeehouses of New Orleans   10

Part 2 - Roasting, Grinding, Brewing, and Storing

Roasting for Freshness   15
Grinding and Brewing   16
Storing   19

Part 3 - Drinking and Enjoying

Categories and Flavors   23
Coffee Drinks   25
The Coffee Market   28
Consumption   30
Proliferation of Coffeehouses   33

References   39
Contacts   43
Index   45

Tables

1   Arabica Coffee   24
2   Robusta Coffee   25
3   Coffee-Handling (1991)   31

Dedication

To Boris, Beet, Sylvester, and Chatgris who, although they don't drink coffee, are loved nonetheless.

Acknowledgments

Many thanks go to everyone who participated in my persistent interviews, discussions, and nonstop queries about coffeehouses and the coffee industry. I toast them with a double grande latte.

From the Author

This book represents a collection of facts (and some legend) on the history and popularity of coffee and coffeehouses. This research by no means represents a complete description of coffees, equipment, or coffeehouses; the reader is referred to the References and Contacts section for more detailed information.

When I began research on this project, only several gourmet coffeehouses existed in New Orleans. Consequently, the focus of my early research depended largely on personal experiences and explorations while traveling throughout Europe, Mexico, and six provinces of Canada. And it was the Pacific Northwest that offered a plethora of resources since this area is considered by some to be the "founder of the gourmet coffeehouse" business.

Throughout the decade, however, New Orleanians' love of coffee—combined with the prominence of being the home of the world's largest bulk handling plant—coffeehouses grew in New Orleans at a phenomenal rate. Independent houses opened across the city and chains were formed and sold successful franchises. And outside chains also took advantage of the growing market for coffeehouses in the Crescent City.

I hope you find the historic and contemporary information in *Coffee and Coffeehouses: A Local and International History* interesting and thought-provoking.

Gary Michael Smith
January 1999

Part 1

A History Lesson

The role of coffeehouses in modern America has been one of artistic as well as commercial cooperation between patrons and entrepreneurs alike. One function that many coffeehouses provide today is that of offering a nonalcoholic alternative form of socializing in a time of widespread promotion of alcohol consumption. Another function is to offer artistic expression, in front of an audience, in the form of literary readings, art exhibits, theatrical performances, video and film screenings, fashion shows, and musical performances covering the spectrum of jazz, gospel, bluegrass, old-time country, pop, and rock.

Coffeehouses in Europe have been a mainstay in these relaxed cultures for centuries, and it has only been within the last decade or so that socializing in this venue has become popular throughout America. Popularity is so widespread in fact that today coffee is second only to oil as the largest traded commodity in the world.

The History of Coffee

The names for coffee in almost every country are descended from the Arabian word *qahwa*, meaning "that gives strength," and its Turkish derivative, *kahveh*. The French and Spanish *café*, the Italian *caffè*, the German *kaffee*, the Finnish *kahvi*, the Dutch *koffie*, the Greek *kafes*, and others are all phonetic approximations of the original Arabic or Turkish words. By 1650, the words *coffey* and *coffee* were established out of this profusion of names, and by 1700 the

A History Lesson

single word "coffee" had passed into the language.

The story of coffee is claimed by legend to begin around 800 A.D. with Kaldi, a young goat herder on the hillsides of Yemen, a port on the Arabian Peninsula across from Ethiopia. Kaldi was puzzled by the curious behavior of his goats; every morning they would dash to the many evergreen shrubs scattered throughout the pasture. And these particular bushes were laden with clumps of red berries. After a brief time, the goats would begin to frolic—uncontrollably. Overtaken with curiosity, Kaldi tried the berries himself and soon was dancing along with his goats.

Meanwhile, the monks living in the hills observed this morning ritual and began to deduce there must be something in those little red berries. They experimented and soon discovered that by soaking the beans in water and drinking the broth it kept them awake during nightly prayers.

This goat story may or may not be true, but according to history, coffee was being cultivated in Yemen as long ago as the 6th century. And by the 9th century the Arabs were using coffee beans for nutritional and medicinal purposes.

After coffee's emergence in Arabia, its production was kept under watchful eyes; although Arabia willingly exported large quantities, they nonetheless guarded its cultivation. At one to two pounds of ground coffee per tree, coffee was extremely valuable. And even though a coffee tree can produce for 40 to 50 years, the greatest produce is yielded between the age of 5 to 13 years.

This cautiousness, however, was a losing struggle with European botanists who spied on these Arabian plantation activities. By 1690, the Dutch succeeded in transporting plants out of Arabia and into botanical gardens in Holland. They also began cultivation on the Indosesian island of Java, and in 1706 Javanese coffee arrived in Amsterdam. Thereafter, the Dutch sent coffee plants to botanical gardens throughout Europe.

But acceptance of this new stimulating beverage was not worldwide. From the 13th to 15th centuries, coffeehouses in some areas were labeled dens of immorality and vice. One punishment mandated by the Grand Visier Kuprili of the Turkish Ottoman Empire for those who violated his restriction of coffeehouses were severe beatings for first offense. But the second offense entailed being sewn into a leather bag and thrown into a river. And more harsh treatments were also administered. In the 16th and 17th centuries, for instance, anyone caught drinking coffee in Turkey was put to death. But soon after finding its way from Turkey to Italy, coffee was baptized by Pope Clement VIII, causing a widespread growth of what was known in 15th-century Mecca as the "drink of Islam."

In 17th century Paris, King Louis XIV tried some of the brew during one of his trading trips to Yemen and

A History Lesson

immediately fell in love with it. The Dutch, wanting to please the coffee-loving king, presented him with a single coffee tree. And by the 18th century, Dutch coffee was a bartered luxury in homes in the remote Highland sea lochs of Scotland.

Also in Paris, a government botanist constructed a hot house where the heat and humidity replicated the Yemen climate. To begin the cultivation, a seedling coffee tree was shipped in the early 1720s to Martinique (today, the sister city of New Orleans) in the Caribbean where the French had land and trade interest. But turbulent storms almost destroyed the ship, and most of the cargo was lost. However, the captain, Gabriel Mathieu de Clieu, knew the importance of the small freight and protected the seedling until they reached the island. This seedling, and its progeny, eventually became the rootstock for all South American coffees.

While these French/South American plants were still in the early growing phases, the Dutch already had been quite successful in growing coffee on Java. The French, having a trade route that stopped on the island, then began shipping from the port of Java. And with this new source of coffee at a cheaper price than in Yemen—and with the developing coffee plantations on Bourbon—France's love for coffee grew wildly.

When King Louis the XIV arrived in North America, he founded an intense shipping port called New Orleans. One of the first ships to be unloaded, directly across the street from today's Kaldi's Coffeehouse and Coffeemuseum, carried bags of coffee from two ports: the Yemen port of Mocha and the Indonesian port of Java. In New Orleans, these two coffees were blended together, and the resulting Mocha Java became an instant hit.

The History of Coffeehouses

When and where the first coffeehouse was opened is widely disputed. One theory is that during the 1683 siege of Vienna, Austria the Viennese burned what they thought was camel fodder left behind by the retreating Turks. A well-trained interpreter/courier/spy with the liberating Polish army realized from the aroma that what they were burning were sacks of green coffee beans.

Franciszek Jerzy Kulczycki claimed the sacks of coffee from the city council as his reward for leading the Polish Army to the rescue of the city. Kulczycki eventually founded what is believed to be the first *kaffeehaus* in Vienna called The Blue Bottle. Today, there are more than 800 coffeehouses in the city. And even though the name of an establishment often is written as two words, "coffeehouse" is the first (preferred) listing in Webster's II New Riverside University Dictionary, indicating that, perhaps, the one-word term has worked its way into our lexicon.

Another theory on the establishment of the first coffeehouse is based on records in Edinburgh, Scotland. These archives chronicle that John's Coffee House, popularly known as "Peaches," was first opened in the Piazza at the

A History Lesson

northeast of Parliament Close in 1688.

In Paris, cafés are credited with fostering the intellectual ferment that led to the French Revolution; in 1843 there were more than 3,000 cafés in Paris alone. These first coffeehouses tended to attract people of high social standing, such as poets, painters, sculptors, and politicians. The popularity of coffeehouses spread to London, and individual coffeehouses became known for the type of business that was conducted under their roofs. Lloyd's of London originated with Edward Lloyd's Coffee House around 1688, and the London Stock Exchange was the motivator behind Johnathan's Coffee House.

The first coffeehouse in England was opened in Oxford in 1637 and became an integral part of intellectual, social, and commercial life where patrons could discuss literary, political, and mercantile affairs. Also, the rise in coffeehouses corresponded with the rise of the London press and people could read newspapers at the houses. And despite Charles II's attempts to shut them down, the number of coffeehouses multiplied enormously during the Restoration. By 1700, there were nearly 2,000 coffeehouses in London, or one for every 300 or 400 Londoners.

Even then, coffeehouses were attracting an eclectic group who enjoyed intellectualizing on numerous topics. But King Charles II of England outlawed coffeehouses when he noticed that both upper and lower classes were mingling together. Consequently, he referred to these places as "penny universities."

Coffeehouses also were convenient centers for sending and receiving mail in days when government efforts to develop a postal system were futile because of the absence of street numbers. In the 1637 Oxford coffeehouse, anybody willing to pay the one penny entrance fee could join in the discussions that went on continuously. This, too, could be the basis behind the name, since these "entrance by admission" coffeehouses also became known as penny universities. It is from these fragments of history that the Penny Post Coffeehouse in New Orleans most likely acquired its name.

Luckily, coffeehouses in the United States usually do not operate on the two-tier system like many European establishments. Here, patrons can expect to sit, relax, and enjoy a peaceful cup of java. In Italy, however, patrons often opt to stand at a counter, balancing the demitasse cup and baked pastries, instead of paying double for the privilege of sitting at a table.

Even though today traditional coffeehouses are specialty shops serving gourmet coffees and teas, in colonial America the coffeehouse was actually a combination tavern/inn/coffeehouse where coffee, tea, ale, and rum were consumed. Coffeehouses in modern America, though, also can include sleek, high-profile spaces that offer specialty coffee mainly as a tantalizing draw for business but actually prefer to sell to a crowd interested in a more substantial variety of cuisine and, in some establishments, alcohol.

A History Lesson

Early Coffee-Making

Street vending has its beginnings in 17th century Europe when coffee merchants, called "aquacedratjos," actually wore on their clothing all the paraphernalia needed to prepare and serve a fresh cup of coffee. The aquacedratjos peddled their brew from house to house giving their patrons the choice of using their own cups or those of the vendor.

Coffee had become so popular by the mid-1800s that cafés could not keep up with the demand. To help meet the public's mania the first espresso machines were invented by either Louis Bernard Rabaut or Michel Varnier sometime around 1822 in France. And at the Paris Exposition of 1855, Edward Loysel de Santais unveiled his coffee machine astounding the crowds by producing 2,000 cups of bad coffee in one hour. By 1903 a gentleman in Milan by the name of Bezzara introduced the first commercially manufactured machine that could make espresso, although it was not until 1946 that Achille Gaggia designed the prototype for today's machines. The Gaggia machine used hot water under pressure rather than steam, and the first smooth, rich cup of espresso was created.

Early Coffeehouses of New Orleans

Perhaps the reason New Orleans got its reputation as a coffee-consuming capital is because coffee is not a new beverage to this area. Early records show that in 1802 New

Orleans, 1,438 bags of coffee were imported from Latin American. And this number grew to 530,000 bags by 1857. Moreover, the 1858 city directory listed more than 500 coffeehouses in New Orleans. Consequently, it is no wonder that in the 1840s New Orleans was the second largest port in the country—with New York being first—and the fourth largest in the world.

And New Orleanians took full advantage of this standing. A coffee break was scheduled daily from 1800 to 1860 where Creole bankers, brokers, importers, and exporters conducted business on Exchange Alley in the French Quarter in "exchanges," as coffeehouses were called.

It was in this area—from Canal Street to the Place d' Armes—that in 1859 the Sazerac Coffee House was opened by importer John B. Schiller. The coffeehouse was located at 13 Exchange Alley and was named after Schiller's favorite brand of cognac.

Another of the original coffeehouses in this city, Café du Monde, has occupied the same location on Decatur Street since 1862. And near there was one of the first coffee warehouses, where Kaldi's Coffeehouse and Coffeemuseum is located today.

Also historic, Morning Call was established in 1870 by a Yugoslavian immigrant, Joseph Jurasich, at St. Phillip and Decatur streets. The menus of both places have remained unchanged, and although Morning Call moved to a suburb in 1974, it still is operated by the original family—the grandson of the founder.

A History Lesson

And even with the intense competition among the city's brokers, importers, wholesalers, and roasters, the New Orleans Men's Association—later called the Green Coffee Association—was formed and held its first meeting at Galatoire's restaurant on December 20, 1915.

So the coffee industry was well established in the city by the turn of the century. And by 1942, records showed that commerce was thriving in this area with 40 importers, two wholesalers, two storage companies, and eight roasters.

Part 2

Roasting, Grinding, Brewing, and Storing

Roasting for Freshness

Today's coffee drinkers have developed a sophistication in their taste for coffee, and with competition among coffeehouses so great—many of which actually roast as well as grind and brew their drinks—some proprietors demand a high level of freshness. Many coffeehouse owners today require their suppliers to vacuum pack their beans within 30 minutes of roasting, and this coffee must be sold within seven days or it will be thrown away. Some proprietors will even hire a personal roastmaster who is familiar with the roasting properties of the certain coffee beans offered at the owner's coffeehouse.

Coffee roasting equipment, some believe, is an essential part of the coffee business. One coffeehouse in New Orleans uses a 1928 Gothot roaster—one of about 20 in existence today—which takes between 15 and 30 minutes to roast 17 pounds of coffee. And proprietors feel that roasting such a small amount at a time, as opposed to commercial coffee roasting factories that use water to cool hot beans, enables roasters to more closely monitor all processes involved from roasting to air cooling.

The act of roasting is what gives the coffee its essence by transforming sugars, starches, and fats into coffee oil, which really is not an oil but some of the more than 600 compounds that have been drawn to the surface of the bean. And the longer the roasting time the greater the amount of oil brought to the surface, making the ground and brewed coffee smoother than lighter roasts, for which much of the acid is still within the bean. This is why a cup of light roast used to make espresso will be bitter.

Also, dark roast coffees—beans that have been roasted for a longer period of time—have less caffeine and acidity, and when used to make espresso, have even less than regularly brewed coffee because the process of making espresso results in leaving more caffeine in the grounds. Moreover, arabicas, which are used for espresso, contain only half the caffeine of robustas.

Grinding and Brewing

Grinding is an important aspect in the preparation of well-brewed coffee. The coffee for espresso is ground finer than filtered coffee, but not too finely nor too coarsely. If the coffee is ground too finely, the water will take too long to drain, making the coffee bitter; if ground too coarsely, the water will pass over the coffee too quickly, not allowing the oils to be extracted and making the coffee too weak. Also, the finer the grind, the greater the chance of damaging the flavor oils of the bean. In general, the grounds should be fine and gritty, but not powdery; the appropriate size could be compared with sugar or salt.

Although one could use a mortar and pestle to grind beans, the preferred way today is to use either a good burr grinder with a powerful, slow-speed motor than generates little heat; heat generated by grinding is an easy way to destroy the flavor of coffee. And be advised that most grocery store grinders do not grind finely enough for good espresso, even if set on the finest setting.

Today's espresso is different from filtered coffee in several ways. Filtered coffee is a clear liquid that contains only a small amount of solid material. Espresso, on the other hand, contains solids suspended in liquid, dissolved solids, and oils broken down by heat.

Many people believe that espresso is loaded with caffeine, but in reality, full caffeine extraction is impossible because of the extremely fast brewing period. The sensation of stronger coffee is a result of the reaction of the taste buds, which open much wider and faster because of the increased temperature of the liquid. This physiological reaction enables the caffeine to enter the body quicker without the acidity (and nervousness) associated with regular coffee. Espresso—although possessing half the caffeine as regular brewed coffee—is stronger because it packs the same amount of coffee and suspended solids into one to two ounces of water instead of the typical six to ten ounces.

Moreover, by comparison a cup of regular robusta (supermarket) coffee contains as much as 150mg of caffeine whereas a cup of espressos made from arabica beans has only about 60 to 90mg. And dark roast contains even less caffeine.

Also, an espresso machine creates a pressure of 9x gravity, and the water should be 184 to 189 degrees

Fahrenheit as it leaves the spout. The water temperature in the tank meanwhile is around 230 degrees. Consequently, few home machines can perform up to the standards of commercial machines; it would cost a consumer about $400 for an authentic home espresso outfit, unless of course you wanted to pay up to $17,000 for a hammered copper and brass Faema or a LaCimbali machine from Italy.

But even a good counter top machine can produce good quality espresso and cappuccino, if done correctly. Without going into too much detail on frothing (other texts give more information), basic rules to follow include those listed below.

- Use only cold milk. It froths easier than warm or even room temperature milk.

- Use nonfat milk for a stiff, dry foam, or 2 percent or whole milk for a smoother, creamier, longer-lasting head.

- Use a stainless steel pitcher, not ceramic or glass. There's something about the steel vibrating while frothing that makes the task easier.

With regard to brewing regular coffee, remember that coffee loses its flavor quickly, so reheating on a stove or in a microwave is never recommended unless you have a taste for stale coffee. Also, the brew basket should be removed immediately after brewing because the residual dripping coffee is bitter. Finally, impatient office workers should be discouraged from replacing the pot with their cup during the brew cycle; this disturbs the balance of the whole pot of coffee.

Storing

Storage of ground coffee or whole beans also is important to maintain the quality of the flavor. Although only whole beans should be stored, there is controversy over whether or not to freeze. Experts say that since coffee oil is water soluble, it will freeze—especially since, from the extended roasting time, much of it is on the surface of the bean. And some feel that once the oils and aromatics are congealed by being frozen, they are never the same.

Some good rules of thumb for storing coffee are a) store only the amount of beans that can be used within a week to 10 days, b) freeze only if you plan of keeping it longer than two weeks, and c) don't even bother storing grounds since they begin to stale immediately after grinding and will absorb odors from the refrigerator. And to prevent freezer burn of beans, stored only in a glass, airtight container; this will minimize air contamination.

For the best results, though, coffee should be stored in a cool, dark, and dry place, and use within a few days.

Part 3

Drinking and Enjoying

Categories and Flavors

The two major commercial categories of coffee sold in this country are Coffea arabica and Coffea canephora (robusta), and each has its own characteristics and place of origin. Arabica beans are hard and more flavorful than robusta beans, are grown at higher altitudes, and used to make the gourmet coffees. The robusta bean is less fragile, hardier, less expensive, and as mentioned earlier contains twice the caffeine as arabicas. This is the coffee that is sold in grocery stores.

Grading involves such criteria as size, color, species, cup quality, the altitude at which it is grown, and the process used for gathering and for preparation. Some examples are displayed in tables 1 and 2 below.

Some gourmet beans may differ from imported beans in that many are flavored. These flavors do not come naturally but are given to the bean by way of a liquid flavor essence bath after roasting, whereby the bean absorbs the flavors until saturated. Some of the most popular flavors include French Vanilla, Amaretta, Brazilian Oro, Viennese, Toasted Almond, Irish Cream, Hazelnut Cream, Mocha Java, Southern Pecan, French Praline, and Bananas Foster. Flavored syrups also are popular in flavoring both lattes and even just steamed milk with no espresso.

But even if you cannot find your preferred flavor of bean at your favorite coffeehouse, you can buy the beans whole at coffee stores such as the Orleans Coffee Exchange.

ARABICA (GOURMET COFFEE)	
Location	**Coffee**
Kenya	AA
Tanzania	Kilimanjaro
Celebes (Holland)	Sulawesi
Costa Rica	Tarrazu
Guatemala	Antigua
Brazil	Bourbon Santos
Venezuela	Maradcaibo, Tachira
Peru	Chanchamayo
Jamaica	Blue Mountain
Yemen	Mocha, Sanani
Hawaii	Kona
India	Mysore
El Salvador	Euro Prep
Mexico	Coatepec, High Grown Daxaca Pluma
Ethiopia	Harrar, Yergacheffe
New Guinea	"Y" Grade
Colombia	Supremo

Table 1. Arabica Coffee

ROBUSTA ("SUPERMARKET" COFFEE)	
Location	Coffee
Indonesia	Java
India, Uganda	Drugar, Wugar
The Ivory Coast	Grade 1

Table 2. Robusta Coffee

The Exchange, located in the French Quarter beneath an apartment once occupied by playwright Tennessee Williams, offers more than 100 different flavors of coffee from 22 different countries including New Guinea, Jamaica, Peru, and Malawi (Fine Wash Malawi). And many coffeehouses even concoct their own combinations of coffee blends, and will eagerly make a cappuccino or espresso with any bean of any flavor.

Coffee Drinks

Although the names and spelling for coffee drinks can be influenced by geographics (a German coffeehouse in Cozumel, Mexico called the Café Caribe offers a *capuchino*), there are different concoctions of espresso as well. *Espresso ristretto* is the same amount of coffee distilled into just less than one ounce of water, while an *espresso macchiato* is a shot

Drinking and Enjoying

of espresso "marked" with a tablespoon of frothed milk.

Cappuccino is somewhat different from espresso. As legend has it, the Capuchin monks were quick to pick up the coffee habit because during the long hours of prayer, the temptation to drift off was irresistible. Muslim traders brought them the Yemen Moka beans, roasted into an eye-opening brew that unfortunately was too strong—and bitter.

By way of a practical joke, a certain Brother Ibio was tripped while carrying a full bucket of sweet cream. The cream splashed into another brother's cup of coffee, and without noticing what had happened the unsuspecting brother drank the coffee and cream mixture. The blend was much more pleasing and thus the brothers found the perfect compliment for their revitalizing brew.

Travelers who stopped to rest at the monastery shared in the monk's pleasure, and the word spread. Coincidentally, the Capuchin monks wore a brown habit topped with a white cowl, which resembled their beloved drink. Today, *cappuccino* consists of one-third espresso, one-third hot steamed milk, and one-third frothed milk.

Another coffee creation is *latte*, which is the Italian word for milk, and was discovered by an Italian dairy farmer. His youngest son was ill, and the local custom was to give an excess of hot water to the infirm to "steam away the evil spirits." But the farmer had no water close at hand, so he put milk in a kettle over the fire pit. The son drank his fill of the hot milk, and the farmer poured the remainder into his cup of coffee to avoid wasting it. Being pleased with the resulting mixture, he soon was sharing his new drink with his neighbors.

Today, latte is made with steamed milk and very little or no foam and poured into a tall glass. A single espresso is slowly added and drifts to the bottom of the glass. The oils in the coffee determine where the mass is suspended. *Latte macchiato* consists of steamed and frothed milk marked with a tablespoon of espresso dripped through the foam.

Even though New Orleans has a reputation as a major coffee importer, the types of coffee drinks are limited in comparison with other coffee consuming areas such as Seattle; Victoria, British Columbia; and Anchorage, Alaska. Macchiato is common in these places as is *breve*, which uses half and half instead of regular whole, low-fat, or fat-free milk. Consequently, a drinker would have no problem ordering a special combination such as a latte macchiato breve, which is extremely popular in Alaska.

Although cappuccino was enjoyed in France, many Parisians desired a lighter drink for their breakfast meal. A milder brew was found by adding steamed milk to a half cup of cappuccino, making *café au lait*. Some coffeehouses and restaurants today serve café au lait as a half cup of regular brewed coffee and a half cup of steamed milk.

Ice coffee is another phenomenon that seems like an oxymoron, but actually is quite popular—especially in warmer climates. Although any coffee guide can describe the proper equipment and process, it should be noted that some houses will make iced coffee by pouring hot espresso over ice, instead of the traditional—and slower—way of "brewing" slow-drip coffee by dripping room-temperature water through grounds.

It was even discovered prior to the turn of the century that liquor can be mixed successfully, and tastefully, with coffee. New Orleans, ever the party town, developed an alcoholic coffee drink as far back as the 1890s. A "café brûlot diabolique" was served at Antoine's restaurant and contained a mixture of coffee, brandy, and spices. This drink later became a popular way to disguise alcohol during prohibition.

The Coffee Market

Gourmet coffee consumption has caught on so well in this country that curb-side cappuccino—made from such trendy blends as Sumatran, Ethiopian, and Costa Rican—are dispensed from $2,900 Italian-made Caramali espresso machines mounted on $13,000 push carts. Vendors with such high-end equipment can be found on Fifth Avenue and Wall Street in Manhattan, and is so popular that the whole business is unaffected by New York laws attempting to crack down on sidewalk vendors.

Seattle as well seems to be immune to legal harassment in the curb-side vending business. Coffee carts dot downtown Seattle sidewalks, one or two on every corner and are parked outside grocery stores and in the shopping malls of suburbia. One chain even operates two kinds of stores—a fast-paced espresso bar where coffee is poured from patented beer-like taps, and another that serves coffee by the cup, offers counter seating, and sells fresh coffee beans and brewing gear such as the cafetiere pot, espresso and cappuccino machines, and French coffee jugs.

One enterprising couple in New Orleans pioneered a coffee vehicle, by converting a van into a mobile coffee counter that can park downtown in a variety of areas with heavy foot traffic. And celebrities, as well, are cashing in on this new wave of specialized socializing; actress Glenn Close, her sister Jessie Close, and writer Barbara Moss once owned the Leaf & Bean in Boseman, Montana.

It is believed that this craze actually may have started in Seattle in Pike Place Market amid produce stall proprietors, fish market workers, and craftspeople. A sidewalk café in Pioneer Square offers such interesting blends as Guatemalan Antigua and Ethiopian Yergacheffe for a tangy espresso. Seattle still has the traditional coffee shops, though, in such areas as First Avenue among the eclectic mix of business suits and Birkenstocks. And some houses even make iced coffee by pouring hot espresso over ice, instead of the traditional—and slower—way of "brewing" slow-drip coffee by dripping room-temperature water through grounds.

Even though coffee drinking is most often thought of as a relaxing social diversion, as a commercial venture the coffeehouse is a serious business. The Specialty Coffee Association of America (SCAA) is one of three trade organizations in the U.S. concerned with coffee, and specifically with specialty coffee. As part of SCAA affiliation, members can tour coffee-growing countries to get first-hand information about the coffee industry. The SCAA also hopes to establish technical standards for roasting and brewing coffee.

Consumption

According to the National Coffee Association 1997 Winter Coffee Drinking Study, 49 percent of the United States' population drinks coffee daily, with men drinking 1.7 cups to 1.5 cups for women. But only 37 percent drink their coffee black while as many as 63 percent add a sweetener and/or cream, milk, or a non-dairy substitute.

It may seem unusual that coffeehouses have proliferated in a city like New Orleans, known probably as one of the most popular party towns in this hemisphere. In the past several years, though, the coffeehouse scene has experienced dramatic growth here. Even though the people of Finland are presently, per capita, the largest group of coffee consumers in the world, according to syndicated market research of grocery store sales New Orleanians consume 1½ times more coffee than the average city-dweller. And the coffee is brewed stronger here as well. The average consumer in other states will use about 1.5 ounces of coffee to make a standard pot, while coffee lovers in Louisiana use at least twice that much to brew the same amount.

To keep up with this demand, 250,000 tons of coffee

moved through the Port of New Orleans in 1989 making the second largest haul of any port in the U.S., the Port of New York and New Jersey being first and second, respectively, in 1989 and 1990. In 1991, the Port of New Orleans moved to first place as shown in table 3 below.

COFFEE HANDLING (1991)		
City	Tonnage	Bags
New Orleans	322,000	5,499,858
New York	212,438	3,628,498
San Francisco	145,130	2,478,870

Table 3. Coffee-Handling (1991)

As can be seen, New Orleans is responsible for handling a fairly good share of the beans shipped into U.S. ports. And it should not be surprising that a portion of this haul stayed in New Orleans to supply one of the best-known coffee centers in the world.

Consequently, to keep flavor and freshness to the optimum, much coffee is roasted in the eight plants in and around New Orleans. At the time of this writing, these roasting plants include PJ's Coffee and Tea Company; Folger Coffee Company; Luzianne Coffee Company; Nestlé/Hills Brothers Coffee Company; International Coffee Corporation; Coffee Roasters of New Orleans; Try-Me Coffee Mills; Covington Coffee Works; and Community Coffee Company, a distributor that also roasts their beans in a plant in Port Allen, Louisiana for their CC's Gourmet Coffee House chain.

The recent development of the bulk handling business may help New Orleans maintain its status of being the number one coffee port in the country. As of May 1993, this city now operates the first, largest, and most versatile U.S. bulk coffee plant in operation in the world—Silocaf of New Orleans, Inc.

Currently, 100,000 pounds of beans an hour slide across the conveyors at Silocaf. Here, both old and new forms of shipment are used: traditional bags that hold either 132 pounds or 154 pounds, the relatively new 2,000-pound plastic super sacks, and the 15-ton cargo containers protected by a plastic liner. And 203 bins hold a maximum capacity of 90 million pounds of beans. A similar bulk handling operation in Trieste, Italy has a capacity of about 10,000 tons—or 20 million pounds—in the bins. The New Orleans plant processed 241,000 tons of beans in 1995 alone.

Overconfidence in the coffee industry should be avoided, however. Even though the National Coffee Association says that nationwide total coffee sales reach about $6.5 billion a year, some experts say that the business already is only a shadow of what it once was. Locally, there used to be coffee traders up and down Magazine and Gravier streets, but today many of them are gone, having been replaced by large European companies with offices in New York.

The head of a New Orleans coffee association explains

that national consumption is flat, if not losing ground. He gives such reasons as health concerns, coupled with the growing popularity of teas, designer soft drinks, and other beverages. Per capita, coffee consumption has been declining for more than 20 years, and the only segment of the market that is showing any growth is specialty coffees with numerous coffeehouses springing up throughout the city and suburbs. And although an ex-Starbucks roastmaster opened The Daily Planet Espresso Bar in the early '90s, Barnes and Noble bookstore in the New Orleans suburb of Metairie features a Starbucks coffee counter and was followed by the Starbucks company, which set up its first coffeehouse in late 1998 in Uptown New Orleans.

Proliferation of Coffeehouses

The number of coffeehouses has dramatically increased in the past several years, offering ambiance ranging from a form of neo-beatnik to a European-style slickness. There could be several reasons for this local growth phenomenon. Some say that patrons are attracted to the casual, and sometimes seedy, atmosphere of coffeehouses, particularly the ones considered by purists to be authentic because they serve coffee and tea only, as opposed to the homogenized, suburban, and sometimes more expensive "restaurants" that simply put the words "coffeehouse," "coffee shop," "café," or "bistro" in the establishment's name. Also, the coffeehouse seems to be a result of neo-prohibitionism among high-school-age youths who prefer this alternative to nightclubs as social meeting places.

Caffeine seems to be more socially acceptable than alcohol because if too much caffeine is consumed, socially unacceptable behavior does not usually follow as does with alcohol. Large amounts of coffee can be consumed and the drinker will only feel tense. Consequently, older singles seem to appreciate the opportunity to meet other "sober" singles.

Some coffeehouses have a variety of attractions such as being combined with a book store as well as having pastries baked on the premises. Some creative establishments such as Coffee Bean in Metairie, Louisiana use their many feet of floor space as a book store, restaurant, and coffeehouse while others such as Cyrano's in Anchorage, Alaska add a theatrical playhouse and art film theater.

Where music is concerned, New Orleanians are open to any opportunity to play or listen to original works. The more progressive coffeehouses inherently have provided an outlet for beginning musicians to show their talent, and occasionally some performers make it to the big time. For example, Emily Salliers of the folk group Indigo Girls gave musical performances at the Penny Post Coffeehouse (now called Neutral Ground Coffee House) on Danneel Street in Uptown New Orleans early in her career. And audiences at Lena Spencer's Caffè Lena in Saratoga Springs in Upstate New York experienced the early works of such icons as Arlo Guthrie, Bob Dylan, Spalding Gray, David Bromberg, and Bruce (Utah) Phillips.

In New Orleans, it seems ironic that a place known for its slow pace and southern flair for the low-pressure, easygoing lifestyle can be a big consumer of such a powerful stimulant as coffee. But perhaps one possible reason for the growth of this industry in the Crescent City is that start-up costs for a coffeehouse are about one-third that of opening a full-service restaurant with a license that allows grilling, frying, or liquor. Moreover, this rapid growth may be compared to the influx of local comedy clubs of the past. But the coffeehouse appears to be a more stable business venture, though, since it seems to offer a service that is readily appreciated almost everywhere.

Perhaps another reason for the influx of coffeehouses on New Orleans streets is that traditional restaurants may frown on students, artists, and the after-theater crowd who want only dessert and coffee. Coffeehouses, on the other hand, take advantage of its patrons' love of eating; homemade pastries are probably as big of enticement as are the coffees themselves, and some establishments even go as far as to have these delicacies supplied directly by pastry chefs from well-known training facilities such as John Folse's Culinary Institute.

Moreover, there exists another class of people who simply want a place to study, write, or conduct other business, and not necessarily in private but perhaps surrounded by the eclectic and sometimes eccentric mix of other New Orleans residents. And these students learn quickly which coffeehouse allow you to plug in a laptop computer; other establishment owners and managers claim that the PCs drain too much power, but a more believable reason is that they do not want patrons occupying a table to work on their computer all day long while nursing a single cup of coffee.

Some enterprising entrepreneurs, however, have recognized this need and have developed "cyber cafés." These are coffeehouses that have Internet accounts and a number of computer workstations. They charge customers for time to log on and access cyberspace for browsing the Internet or accessing email. But these Internet cafés often only specialize in either good espresso or good computer equipment; an establishment with both is a good find.

Another possible reason for the growth of coffeehouses in New Orleans in particular could be its ability to receive imports, via rail, highway, and waterway. And even though Brazil provides 30 percent of the world's coffee, more than 60 different species of coffee beans are grown in and shipped from a variety of countries.

The social significance of the coffeehouse may be equal to the coffee itself. The coffeehouse provides what sociologists call "third places"—spots to gather away from home and work. That is the whole idea behind some of these meeting places: you go in and read the paper, and you can discuss anything you want with anybody you want. Coffeehouses provide an experience beyond just drinking coffee: we like to drink it with people we like.

But whatever the reason for the growing number of coffeehouses, this business seems to have found its niche, one carved into a society that thrives on communication and the ever-elusive luxury of leisure time.

References

Arceneaux, Robert. Telephone conversation with author. New Orleans, LA, 11 December 1992.

Barlow, Yvonne. "Espresso on the Run." *Travel-Holiday* February 1989: 100.

Bell, Lydia. "Vienna, Mozart and More in Austria's Capital City." *Times-Picayune* [New Orleans, LA] 24 November 1991: E1, E4 Living.

Benning, Lee Edwards. *The Cook's Tales, Origins of Famous Foods and Recipes*. The Globe Pequot Press, 1992: 155.

Bloom, Jeremy. "Café Society." *New York Times* 19 May 1991, late ed., sec. 2: 31.

Brown, Catherine. *Broths to Bannocks, Cooking in Scotland 1690 to the Present Day*. London: John Murray Ltd, 1991: 15, 24.

Caffè Lena. Dir. Stephen Trombley. Mirageland/International Cinema, 1989. 60 min.

Calamuneri, Nino. Personal interview with author. New Orleans, LA, 2 May 1992.

Castille, Sandie. Telephone interview with author. New Orleans, LA, 24 October 1991.

Collingwood, Harris. "Curbside Coffee for New York's Bon Vivants." *Business Week* 25 July 1988: 41.

"Complaints Close Sidewalk." *Times-Picayune* [New Orleans, LA] 16 March 1992: A-11.

Connick, Harry Jr. Rec. 1987. *Harry Connick, Jr.* Columbia Records, FCT 40702, 1987.

Cooper, Christopher. "Success is a Matter of Style."

References

Times-Picayune [New Orleans, LA] 14 January 1992: A-4.

Drake, Brian. "Shoestring Film Turns Into a Hit." *New York Times* 7 August 1991: B3.

Dreher, Rod. "Filmmaker Linklater Scores Hit with Low-Budget 'Slacker'" *Morning Advocate* [Baton Rouge, LA] 13 September 1991: 1C-2C.

Dunn, Debra. Personal interview with author. New Orleans, LA, 9 February 1991.

Finn, Kathy. "New Coffee Plant To Give N.O. a Lift; Italian Firm Will Turn Old Silo Into Nation's Top Processing Center." *City Business* [New Orleans, LA] 2-15 December 1991: 1, 20.

Hall, John. "Yes! Dupuy Knows Beans About Coffee." Times-Picayune [New Orleans, LA] 12 April 1992: F-1, 4.

Jurich, Nick. *Espresso. From Bean to Cup.* Missing Link Press, 1991: 198 pps.

Keister, Kim. "New Orleans Comeback." *Historic Preservation* January/February 1991: 31+.

Know Your Coffee: A Nestlé Foodservice Guide. Nestlé Foodservice, Croyden, England, 1991: 2.

Kutner, Sanford A. "Grandma Ruth—85 and Working Every Day!!!" *This Week In New Orleans* August 8, 1992: 1.

Laun, Kathleen. "A Lot Goes Into That Cup of Jo Before It Reaches Your Table." *Times-Picayune* [New Orleans, LA] 11 October 1992: 20-21, 40.

Lemann, Bernard, Samuel Wilson, Jr. *Architectural*

Inventory. New Orleans: Pelican Publishing Company, Inc., 1971: 136. Vol. 1 of *New Orleans Architecture*. 2 vols.

Louis, David. *2201 Fascinating Facts*. New York: Greenwich House, 1983: 86.

Manger, René. *Spilling the Beans* Vol. I, Issue 12, August 21, 1992.

———. *Spilling the Beans* Vol. II, Issue 3, November 27, 1992.

Marsh, Michael. Personal interview with author. New Orleans, LA, 9 February 1991.

Molloy, Joanna. "Hot Coffee: Beauties of the Night on Union Square." *New York* 13 August 1990: 40, 43.

Mullener, Elizabeth. "Glory Days: Magazine Street Coming Back." *Times-Picayune* [New Orleans, LA] 15 January 1992: A-9.

Olson, Alison. "Coffee House Lobbying." *History Today* January 1991: 35-41.

Owen, Thompson, Steve Hamilton, Ted Hood. *Uncommon Grounds, A Publication of Kaldi's Coffeehouse and Coffeemuseum* March 1992: 1-9.

Pacorini, Massimo. Fax to author. New Orleans, LA, 12 December 1996.

Paulsen, Eric. "Seattle's Coffee Subculture." *ITN, The Newsletter of the International Television Association* April 1992: 10, 12.

Reiking, Herta. Personal interview with author. Cozumel, Mexico, 13 August 1992.

Roppolo, Jerry. Personal interview with author. New

References

Orleans, LA, 9 February 1991.

Slacker. Dir. Richard Linklater. 16 mm, 97 min. 1989. Detour, Inc.

Snow, Constance. "Café Olé!" *Times-Picayune* [New Orleans, LA] 23 August 1991: 18-20 Lagniappe.

———. "Some Hot Spots for the Coffee Crowd." *Times-Picayune* [New Orleans, LA] 2 November 1990: 33-34 Lagniappe.

Street, Julia. "Dear Julia." *New Orleans Magazine* March 1993: 14.

Vogt, Jenny. "Caffeine Overload May Be Last Socially Acceptable Vice." *Times-Picayune* [New Orleans, LA] 24 September 1991: 1-2 Living.

Voelker, Bill. "Businesswomen Take Gamble on Coffeehouse." *Times-Picayune* [New Orleans, LA] 20 August 1992: D-1, D-2.

Welsh, James. "Ahhhhhh, Coffee." *Times-Picayune* [New Orleans, LA] 21 February 1993: F-1, F-2.

Williams, David. Email to author. New Orleans, LA, 11 December 1996.

Wintergreen, Donna. "Café Society." *Restaurant Hospitality* May 1990: 132-134.

Zimmerman, Curtis. Telephone conversation with author. New Orleans, LA, 11 December 1992.

Contacts

International Coffee Organization
London
United Kingdom
44-1-71-580-8591
44 1-71-850-6129
library@intercaf.win-uk.net

National Coffee Association of America
Coffee Science Source
110 Wall Street
New York, NY 10005
212-344-5596
212-425-7059 fax
http://www.coffeescience.org
info@coffeescience.org

Specialty Coffee Association of America
One World Trade Center, Suite 1200
Long Beach, CA 90831-0800
562-624-4100
562-624-4101 fax
http://scaa.org/scaa/contact.html
coffee@scaa.org

Index

A

Achille Gaggia, 10
Antoine's, 28
aquacedratjos, 10
arabica, 17
arabicas, 16

B

Bezzara, 10
Bourbon, 6
Brazil, 36
breve, 27
bulk coffee plant, 32
    Silocaf of New Orleans, Inc., 32
    Trieste, Italy, 32

C

café au lait, 27
café brûlot diabolique, 28
Café Caribe, 25
Café du Monde, 11
Caffè Lena, 34
caffeine, 17
Cappuccino, 26
Capuchin monks, 26

Index

Brother Ibio, 26
Caramali, 28
categories, 23
    Coffea arabica, 23
    Coffea canephora (robusta), 23
CC's Gourmet Coffee House, 32
Coffee Bean, 34
Coffee carts, 28
Covington Coffee Works, 31
cyber cafés, 36
Cyrano's, 34

D

Dutch, 5

E

Edinburgh, 7
Edward Lloyd's Coffee House, 8
Edward Loysel de Santais, 10
Espresso, 17
espresso bar, 29
Exchange Alley, 11

F

Faema, 18

Filtered coffee, 17
flavors, 23
Franciszek Jerzy Kulczycki, 7
frothing, 18
    2 percent, 18
    nonfat milk, 18
    whole milk, 18

G

Gabriel Mathieu de Clieu, 6
Gothot, 15
Grading, 23
Grand Visier Kuprili, 5
Green Coffee Association, 12
Grinding, 16

I

Ice coffee, 27
Internet cafés, 36

J

Java, 5, 7
John B. Schiller, 11
John Folse's Culinary Institute, 35
Johnathan's Coffee House, 8

Index

John's Coffee House, 7
Joseph Jurasich, 11

K

Kaldi, 4
Kaldi's Coffeehouse and Coffeemuseum, 6
King Charles II, 8
King Louis XIV, 5

L

LaCimbali, 18
laptop computer, 35
Latin American, 11
latte, 26
    Latte macchiato, 27
Leaf & Bean, 29
literary readings, 3
Lloyd's of London, 8
London Stock Exchange, 8
Louis Bernard Rabaut, 10

M

Martinique, 6
Michel Varnier, 10
Mocha, 7

Morning Call, 11

N

National Coffee Association, 30
neo-prohibitionism, 33
Neutral Ground Coffee House, 34
New Orleans Men's Association, 12

O

Orleans Coffee Exchange, 23
Oxford, 8

P

Paris, 8
Paris Exposition of 1855, 10
Parliament Close, 8
Peaches, 7
Penny Post Coffeehouse, 9, 34
penny universities, 8
Pope Clement VIII, 5
Port of New Jersey, 31
Port of New Orleans, 31
Port of New York, 31

R

reheating, 18
restaurants, 33
    bistro, 33
    café, 33
    coffee shop, 33
roasting plants, 31
    Coffee Roasters of New Orleans, 31
    Community Coffee Company, 31
    Folger Coffee Company, 31
    International Coffee Corporation, 31
    Luzianne Coffee Company, 31
    Nestlé/Hills Brothers Coffee Company, 31
    PJ's Coffee and Tea Company, 31
    Try-Me Coffee Mills, 31
roastmaster, 15
robusta, 17
robustas, 16

S

Sazerac Coffee House, 11
Scotland, 6
social significance, 36
    third places, 36
Specialty Coffee Association of America, 29
Starbucks, 33

Barnes and Noble, 33
Storage, 19
    freeze, 19

T

The Blue Bottle, 7
The Daily Planet Espresso Bar, 33
Turkey, 5
Turkish Ottoman Empire, 5

V

Vienna, 7

Y

Yemen, 4, 6

Chatgris Press

Order Form

Date: _____

Publications from Chatgris Press

☐   *The Peer-Reviewed Journal: A Comprehensive Guide through the Editorial Process* (ISBN 0-9658380-0-5) $35 plus $3 for Priority Mail/$6 Global Priority shipping, $1.74 for 4th Class postage, or include Federal Express number (Louisiana residents add $1.40 for sales tax; New Orleans residents add $3.32 for municipal tax.)

☐   *The Complete Guide to Driving Etiquette* (ISBN 0-9658380-1-3) $24.95 plus $3 Priority Mail/$6 Global Priority shipping, $1.24 for 4th Class postage, or include Federal Express number (Louisiana residents add $.99 for sales tax; New Orleans residents add $2.37 for municipal tax.)

☐   *The Veranda* (literary journal of essays and short stories) $3 per issue plus $3 Priority Mail/$6 Global Priority shipping, $1.24 for 4th Class postage, or include Federal Express number (Louisiana residents add $.12 for sales tax; New Orleans residents add $.28 for municipal tax.)

☐   *Coffee and Coffeehouses: A Local and International History* (ISBN 0-9658380-2-1) $7.95 plus $3 Priority Mail/$6 Global Priority shipping, $1.24 for 3rd Class postage, or include Federal Express number (Louisiana residents add $.31 for sales tax; New Orleans residents add $.75 for municipal tax.)

Purchaser Information

Name _____

Title _____

Department _____

Company _____

Address _____

_____

_____

Phone (____) _____ **Fax** (____) _____

Email _____

FedEx # _____

Make check or money order payable to Chatgris Press and mail to Chatgris Press, P.O. Box 15092, New Orleans, LA 70175-5092. For more information, call 504-895-5219 or email gsmith@comm.net.